PRACTICAL CAREERS FOR PRACTICAL PEOPLE

COSMETOLOGIST

Cathleen Small

CHERITON
CHILDREN'S BOOKS

Published in 2026 by **Cheriton Children's Books**
1 Bank Drive West, Shrewsbury, Shropshire, SY3 9DJ, UK

First Edition

Author: Cathleen Small
Designer: Jessica Moon
Editor: Sarah Eason
Proofreader: Ella Short

Picture credits: Cover: Shutterstock/Roman Fenton. Inside: p4: Shutterstock/LightField Studios, p5: Shutterstock/Steklo, p6: Shutterstock/Yakobchuk Viacheslav, p7: Shutterstock/Yakobchuk Viacheslav, p9b: Shutterstock/Ovidiu Hrubaru, p9t: Shutterstock/Dorde Krstic, p10: Shutterstock/Ihor Bulyhin, p11: Shutterstock/Yakobchuk Viacheslav, p12: Shutterstock/Anatoliy Gleb, p13: Shutterstock/Pixel Shot, p14: Shutterstock/Kostiantyn Voitenko, p15: Shutterstock/Pixel Shot, p16: Shutterstock/AS Photo Family, p17: Shutterstock/Kathy Hutchins, p18: Shutterstock/Africa Studio, p19: Shutterstock/Monkey Business Images, p20: Shutterstock/Jose Calsina, p21: Shutterstock/Jocelyne Vautour, p22: Shutterstock/Pixel Shot, p23: Shutterstock/Davide Angelini, p25b: Shutterstock/PeopleImages.com/Yuri A, p25t: Shutterstock/Studio Romantic, p26: Shutterstock/Drazen Zigic, p28: Shutterstock/Pixel Shot, p29: Shutterstock/Hedgehog94, p30: Shutterstock/Pixel Shot, p31: Shutterstock/Shift Drive, p32: Shutterstock/Dorde Krstic, p33: Shutterstock/DS Tkachuk, p34: Shutterstock/Kievstock, p35: Shutterstock/Anatoliy Gleb, p36: Shutterstock/Kostiantyn Voitenko, p37: Shutterstock/D Busquets, p38: Shutterstock/Rawpixel.com, p39: Shutterstock/Antoniodiaz, p40: Shutterstock/Spaskov, p41: Shutterstock/Yakov Oskanov, p42: Shutterstock/Motortion Films, p43: Shutterstock/True Touch Lifestyle, p44: Shutterstock/PeopleImages.com/Yuri A, p46: Shutterstock/Kiomu Studio, p47: Shutterstock/Pixel Shot, p48: Shutterstock/Olesia Bilkei, p49: Shutterstock/Olesia Bilkei, p50: Shutterstock/Puhhha, p51: Shutterstock/Beauty Hero, p52: Shutterstock/New Africa, p53: Shutterstock/Studio Romantic, p54: Shutterstock/Kokulina, p55: Shutterstock/Amedeoemaja, p56: Shutterstock/Monkey Business Images, p57: Shutterstock/MDV Edwards, p59: Shutterstock/New Africa, p63: Shutterstock/Lucky Business.

Printed in China

CONTENTS

CHAPTER 1

Working in the Cosmetology Industry

Thinking about what you want to do for your future career might be daunting. Some people know from an early age what they want to do. Others find themselves in high school still struggling to decide what they want to do when they "grow up." In general, there are two main paths to consider: Do you want to go to college and get a job in a specialized industry in which advanced education is a must? Or are you more focused on a practical career? Perhaps one in which you can get the training you need and start building your career relatively quickly?

Cosmetologist is an in-demand practical career. There is always a need for people who have talent and skills in the beauty industry.

GOOD NEWS FOR PRACTICAL PEOPLE

In recent decades, more and more students have chosen to go to college. If you're someone who leans more toward a practical career, this is great news for you. That's because the increase in people choosing careers that require college has meant there are fewer people going into trades. And that means there are plenty of jobs to be had in various trades.

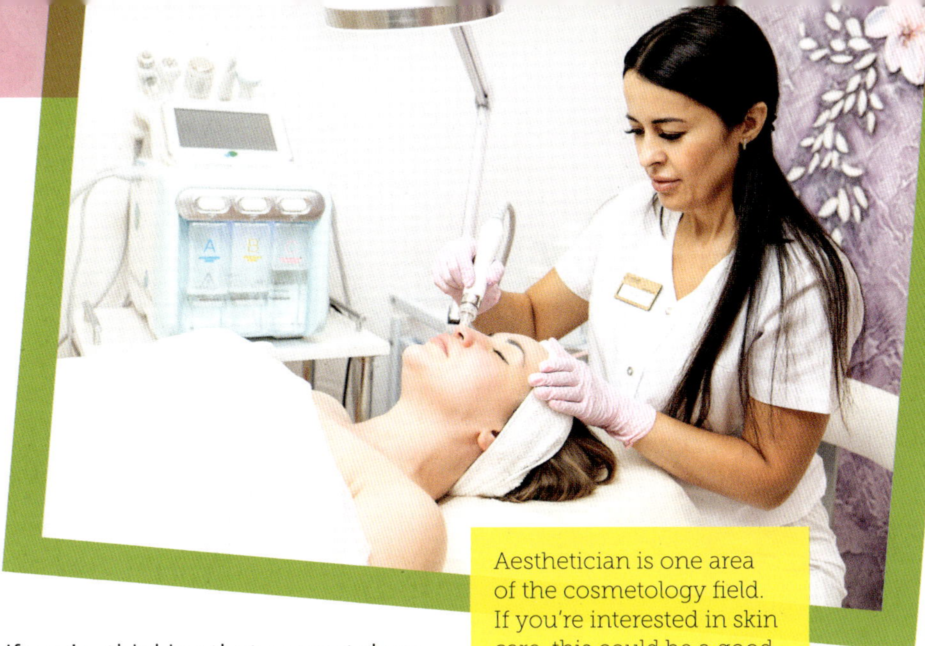

Aesthetician is one area of the cosmetology field. If you're interested in skin care, this could be a good career path for you.

If you're thinking that cosmetology is a career you might enjoy, the good news is that the Bureau of Labor Statistics (BLS) projects a huge increase in employment demand for people in this particular area. In fact, they predict an increase of 8 percent in employment for cosmetologists over the coming decade, which is more than twice the growth rate expected across all occupations in the United States! So there is plenty of opportunity in this area.

THINKING AHEAD

When you're thinking about your future career as a cosmetologist, there are several important factors to carefully consider:

- Do you have skills in a particular part of the cosmetology field—or could you develop them?
- Will the job be secure?
- Will the job likely exist in the future as technology advances and introduces changes to the workplace?
- What is the pay?
- What training is involved, and how much will it cost?
- What benefits does the cosmetology field offer in addition to pay?

We'll explore the answers to all the above questions in this chapter.

IN IT FOR THE LONG TERM

Currently, the average retirement age for American citizens is 64. This means that people of your generation will likely be working for a long time. So it's important to choose your career carefully—you will probably be doing it for many years to come. You want to be sure that you devote the next 40-plus years of your life to something you'll enjoy. So, let's take a look at cosmetology and what this growing career area has to offer you.

TIME TO START PLANNING

You can always change careers later in life if you decide you don't like what you're doing. But making big changes like a career shift can be difficult as you get older. That's why it's good to explore career options now, when you have some time to narrow down what you think you would enjoy doing in the coming decades. Plus, if you want to build financial stability, it's easier to do so if you stick with one field. When you change careers partway through your working life, doing so often requires you to take a sizable pay cut as you start at the bottom of a new career. It also involves a learning curve. Taking less money and having to start over with your training can be difficult to do when you have more responsibilities.

PATHS TO A CAREER IN COSMETOLOGY

The cosmetology field covers a lot of ground. As Emma Long, a member of Paul Mitchell's Advanced Education Style & Texture Team, says, "Cosmetology is the main 'hub' for the beauty industry. Most areas in the beauty world fall under a cosmetology license. It is, in my opinion, the most versatile license in the beauty industry." Indeed it is. Cosmetology includes haircare, skin care, nail care, and makeup. Under the umbrellas of these four main areas of the field are several subspecialities. They include hair coloring and relaxing, facials and waxing, manicures and pedicures, and bridal and runway makeup. There are a vast number of things you can do with a cosmetology license—the options are endless.

Think about which parts of the cosmetology field might suit you. If you are interested in skin care, for example, you could consider a number of roles in this area of the industry.

The most important factor when deciding on any career is whether you will find it fulfilling.

WOULD THE FIELD SUIT YOU?

One of the key questions you need to ask yourself is, would you enjoy being a cosmetologist? Let's look at some aspects of the field that can help you answer that question.

First, do you like interacting with people? As a cosmetologist, you work directly with clients, and interpersonal relationships are very important. Clients are trusting you with their body, and they'll only do so if they trust you as a person. So if you enjoy interacting with people and you are good at setting them at ease, cosmetology could be a really rewarding career field for you.

Second, would you like variety in your job? Even if you specialize in one area of the field, no two jobs are going be the same. No two people have the exact same hair or the exact same wishes for their style. No two people have the same face or the same makeup preferences. Every day is going to be different, and every job within each day will be different. Would you enjoy that type of variety in your work?

Are you looking for a job with a flexible schedule? It is often the case that cosmetologists set their own hours, which is a real benefit if you have other priorities in life that you want to plan around.

WOULD YOU LIKE TO BE YOUR OWN BOSS?

Have you ever thought about someday working for yourself? This is an important question to carefully consider because many cosmetologists are self-employed. They may rent a chair in a salon, or they may work out of their house or at a spa. If being your own boss has some appeal to you, you might enjoy this particular career field.

DO YOU HAVE THE RIGHT SKILLS?

If you're wondering whether you have the right skills to be a cosmetologist, here are some key ones that help contribute to a successful career in the field:

- **Connecting with others:** One important skill to have as a cosmetologist is the ability to connect with people. If you're someone who likes interacting with people, you can do well as a cosmetologist. If you're very introverted and prefer to keep to yourself, that would present a challenge. You will be working with customers all day, and most people are used to being chatty with their hairdresser or aesthetician—and they enjoy it.
- **Physical fitness:** You'll also need to have good physical stamina, since cosmetologists typically spend a lot of time on their feet.
- **Good coordination:** You'll need good dexterity, too, because you'll be working with your hands. This is a practical issue but also a safety concern. If you're a hairdresser, you will work with very sharp scissors, and a slip of the hand could result in a cut to yourself or your client—and damage to your reputation.

SUCCESS STORIES

Ecuador-born Jen Atkin has been named the most influential hairstylist in the world by *The New York Times*. However, she had just $300 and a Honda Civic to her name when she moved to Los Angeles at the age of 19 with dreams of working in the hairstyling industry. She started as a receptionist at a West Hollywood salon, but within seven years she was working as a stylist on the hair team for one of Madonna's tours and working fashion shows in Paris. She styled hair for the Kardashians, Hailey Bieber, Gigi and Bella Hadid, Katy Perry, and many more stars. She has branched out in other entrepreneurial efforts, cofounding the OUAI haircare line and writing columns for *Glamour* magazine. She founded a digital magazine titled *Mane Addicts* and wrote a book. Her 5.3 million Instagram followers know her as @jenatkinhair, and her @JenAtkin YouTube channel offers hair tutorials and more.

Enjoying interaction with others is key to a cosmetology career. You'll be working with people all day, every day, so good people skills are a must.

Jen Atkin (right) has built a very successful career as a hairstylist to the stars.

CREATIVE VISION

Creativity is also a real benefit in the field of cosmetology. Clients will often come to you with an idea of what they want, but your creativity in making their vision come to life is what will set you apart in the field. The same is true with product and industry knowledge. Clients often want to know what products they can use for a particular goal, such as improved skin, and if you know the available products in your field well, it will help to set you apart from the competition.

A CREATIVE JOB

"If you enjoy being creative, there is a lot of scope in this field. There is always room for fun, new ideas and styles."

MANAGING TIME AND AN OPEN MIND

Time-management skills are another requirement. You don't want to rush through a beauty treatment, but if it takes you three hours to do a manicure that another manicurist would do in one hour, you're going to earn significantly less money because you'll be able to see fewer clients. (Not to mention, no client has the patience to sit for a three-hour manicure! People are busy and want their treatment done efficiently—and well.)

And finally, you'll need to be open to learning. Styles change quickly, and you'll want to keep up with the latest trends and developments in the field as it evolves.

Nail technicians and manicurists fall under the umbrella of cosmetologists. Nail art has gotten so creative in recent years that this can be a really fun part of the field.

Facials and skin rejuvenation are just some of the services you would provide if you choose a career as an aesthetician.

IS THERE JOB SECURITY?

There is job security for cosmetologists based on the projections for job outlook in the coming decade. Because jobs in the cosmetology field require a fair amount of physical stamina, too, older professionals in the industry often move into other jobs as they age. That opens plenty of jobs for people new to the industry.

However, one important note is about self-employment. As you've already learned, many cosmetologists are self-employed, which can bring some instability to the job. In cosmetology, your job is as stable as you make it. It's up to you to create stability by being reliable, available to clients, professional, and good at what you do. You need to build a strong, loyal clientele that values your work because they know you're good at what you do. If they know they can count on you, there's job stability in this field. But if you're a person who struggles to be organized and motivated, stability can be challenging when self-employed.

WHAT WILL THE FUTURE BRING?

"What will the future bring?" is the big question in any industry today. Technology and artificial intelligence (AI) are changing rapidly, and that is bringing changes to every field of work. Cosmetology is no exception. One worry people often have is whether these changes will ultimately cost them their jobs. The good news is that's unlikely in the cosmetology industry. The technological advances in the field involve tools that can help cosmetologists work better and more efficiently—not tools that will replace cosmetologists. (We'll talk more about advancements in the field in Chapter 6.) If you're willing to implement new technology in a way that will benefit you and your clients, there is no need to worry that it will harm your career.

There is a lot of earning potential for good hairstylists, especially those working in high-end salons in major cities.

HOW MUCH WILL I EARN?

How much will you earn as a cosmetologist? Well, that's a million-dollar question. And if you're good at what you do, it could literally be a million-dollar question! The hairstylist Jen Atkin charges about $600 for a haircut and she is reportedly worth well over $1 million. But most cosmetologists don't make quite that much money!

The BLS lists the median hourly rates for cosmetologists, rather than annual salaries. That is likely because many cosmetologists work part time. That makes their annual salary lower than that of a full-time cosmetologist.

The BLS lists the median rate for cosmetologists at about $16.87 per hour, which equates to just over $34,000 per year if the cosmetologist works full time. That's below the median annual salary across all occupations, which is around $47,000. But that's not all there is to the story. A cosmetologist's wages are greatly affected by the part of the industry they practice in and the location where they work. For example, in San Francisco it's common for a woman's haircut to cost more than $100—and that doesn't include coloring or highlighting. But in Omaha, Nebraska, even a high-level salon charges about half that. So hairstylists in San Francisco are making far above $16.87 per hour.

LOOKING AT COSTS OF COLLEGE

Another factor in your decision about whether to become a cosmetologist is the cost of other options, such as college. Cosmetologists typically go to school for their trade, depending on which part of the field they're in. However, they don't attend a four-year university program, and that saves them a lot of money.

The Education Data Initiative (EDI) states that the average cost of a four-year college education at an in-state public university in the United States in 2024 was more than $108,000. At an out-of-state university, it was more than $182,000. At a private university, it cost an astounding $234,000. The EDI also notes that the average borrower of student loans spends about 20 years paying them off. That's a lot of money—and a lot of time spent paying off loans!

If you have your sights set on a career that you feel passionate about, and it requires college, then paying hefty college fees is no doubt a good investment. But if what you really enjoy is something more practical, such as cosmetology, a major plus is that you won't have to get into great debt to pay for college.

Trade school will provide a solid foundation in cosmetology.

MORE DETAIL ABOUT COSTS AND COLLEGE OPTIONS

Like most forms of education or training, cosmetology school is not cheap. According to Milady, the average cost of attending cosmetology school in the United States is about $16,251. Most of that amount goes toward cosmetology school itself, though a small part is made up of costs for cosmetology kits and licensing fees.

The average costs for education do vary by state, though. Alaska is typically the least expensive state, with Wyoming, South Dakota, Massachusetts, Kentucky, and a few southern states also being quite reasonable. The most expensive is Nevada, followed by several other states, including California, Virginia, Maryland, and Connecticut.

It is worth investing the time and money in good training so you are fully prepared for the workplace.

Some community colleges offer cosmetology programs, and they are typically less expensive than cosmetology schools. You can even earn a two-year associate's degree in cosmetology if you take the community college route.

RETIREMENT PLANS: YOU SHOULD HAVE ONE!

You're likely not at a stage in your life to be thinking a lot about retirement, but one thing you'll want to do is be positive about starting a retirement plan. Sure, you're giving up part of your pay for something in the distant future—you likely won't touch that money for more than 45 years. But someday, you're going to want to retire, and here's the beauty of retirement plans: they multiply. The earlier you start saving, the more your money multiplies as your investments grow. And the more money you put in, the more it multiplies in turn. When you do reach the point of retirement, you'll be very happy to see all that money you put in—plus all the additional amount you earned on it by investing wisely.

Typically, a community college program will cost more in the region of $5,000—though it varies by college and location. Whichever route you choose, even the most expensive places to attend cosmetology school are far less expensive than paying for a four-year college education.

OTHER BENEFITS TO CONSIDER

Pay is very important, but it isn't everything. It's important to also consider the total compensation package that comes with a job. Total compensation typically includes your salary, any insurance offerings (such as health and life), and any retirement plans.

Because many cosmetologists are self-employed, there may not be any additional benefits to the job over just the salary. However, for cosmetologists who are employed in a more traditional setting—such as an employer-owned spa or salon—there may be health insurance, retirement plans, paid time off, and more.

As you train, you'll discover what areas of the field you most enjoy. You may develop a real passion for makeup, for example.

THE NEED FOR INSURANCE

Insurance is a must-have. There's no law saying you must have health coverage. However, if you're smart, you'll make sure you have it. If you're self-employed, you'll have to acquire your own insurance. You'll also need to set up your own retirement plan if you want one. Again, it's smart to have one, though not required for the job.

Many cosmetologists are self-employed and need to build buying insurance into their plans as they budget for the future.

INSURANCE: AN IMPORTANT CONSIDERATION

We admit that insurance may not seem an exciting topic! However, it's a very important one. You should have health insurance. And if your employer doesn't offer it or if you are self-employed, you'll want to get it.

Health insurance covers you when you need medical or other health-related help. While health insurance can be expensive, you'll be glad you have it if you need an appointment with a doctor or spend time in the hospital, because medical bills add up quickly.

Most states don't require you to have health insurance. However, it is worth noting that in four states—California, Massachusetts, Rhode Island, and New Jersey—and the District of Columbia, you must pay a tax penalty if you can't provide proof of health insurance on your annual tax return. If you live in one of those states or in Washington, DC, you'll want to have health insurance so you can avoid the tax penalty—as well as for your own protection, of course.

Mario Dedivanovic is one of the industry's most in-demand artists.

SUCCESS STORIES

Makeup artist Mario Dedivanovic gained fame as a master of contouring. He's a master of the smoky eye, too. And he also happens to be the Kardashian family's makeup artist of choice. Dedivanovic started at the bottom and worked his way up. He got a job after high school at Sephora, working as a fragrance consultant. On his first day, a woman asked him to help her choose a lipstick. Not long after, two singers came into Sephora for makeup advice, and then hired Dedivanovic to do their makeup for a show. And so at 17 years old, his career as a makeup artist was launched. Since then, he has made-up many celebrities and taught masterclasses. He debuted his makeup line, Makeup by Mario, in 2020, and the line is now valued at more than $200 million. It's estimated that Mario's daily rate for makeup artistry is $30,000. Find him at @makeupbymario on Instagram, where he has 13.9 million followers, and at @makeupbymario on YouTube.

A JOB YOU'LL LOVE

"I used to love creating makeup looks for my friends in high school. One of them said I'd make a great makeup artist, and the idea to turn my passion into a career began there."

CHAPTER 2

Getting Started

If you like what you've learned so far, it's likely that a career as a cosmetologist sounds appealing. Let's look at what you need to do to begin your working life in this sector.

DETERMINE WHAT TRAINING YOU NEED

For virtually any job, you'll need to have a high school diploma or GED. So that's your first step. And while a GED is completely valid, there are some employers who prefer you have a high school diploma. It shows that you can see a path through and finish it. So even though you may be eager to start your career, stay at high school and get that diploma first. And then you can think about the next step, which most likely will include either trade school or community college. For almost every job in the cosmetology field, you need to be licensed, and to be licensed you need to have completed the appropriate schooling or training.

COSMETOLOGY SCHOOL

Cosmetology school covers coursework in haircutting and hairstyling, makeup, nail care, and skin care (aesthetics). In addition, you'll learn about sanitization and

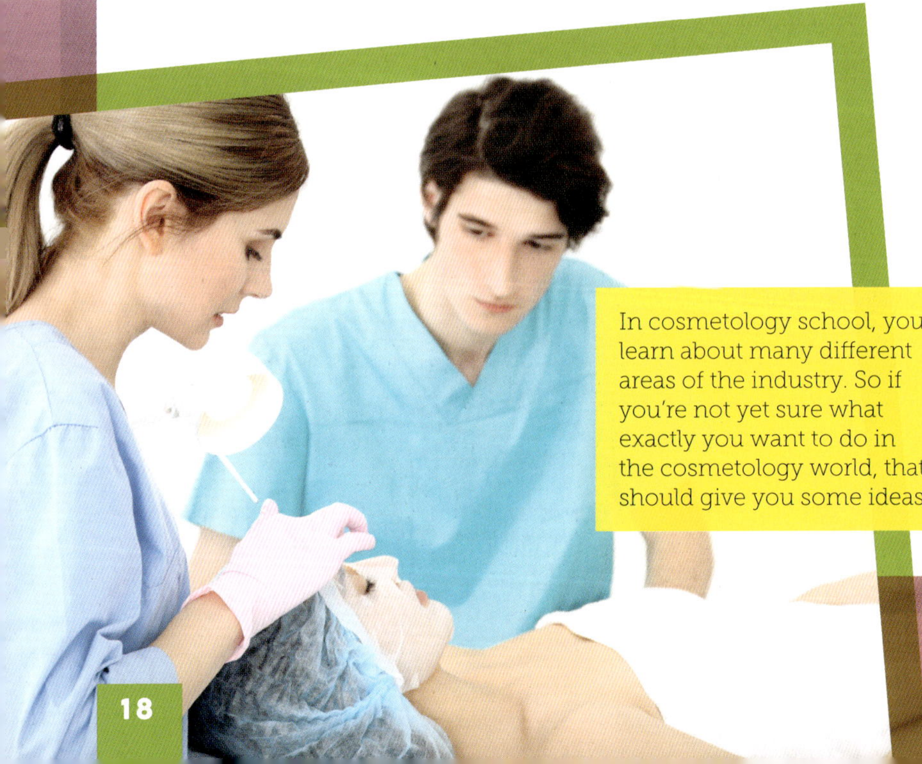

In cosmetology school, you'll learn about many different areas of the industry. So if you're not yet sure what exactly you want to do in the cosmetology world, that should give you some ideas.

In cosmetology classes, you'll learn how to cut, style, color, and care for hair, as well as how to work with extensions.

safety, as well as business and marketing. More specifically, you'll learn the following skills:

- **Haircare:** You will be trained in haircutting, hair coloring, and hairstyling. In addition you'll train in extensions, chemical treatments, and hair care.
- **Makeup:** Training includes color theory to complement skin, eye, and hair tones. You'll learn about facial structures and the makeup techniques that best work for each type. Makeup tools and products are part of the training. Specialized makeup applications for weddings, events, special effects, and photography and movie shoots are included.
- **Nail care:** This includes basic manicure and pedicure techniques, including overlays, artwork, acrylics, and gel nails, as well as nail repair.
- **Skin care:** You'll learn about the skin's anatomy (remember, the skin is an organ—the largest one in the body, in fact). You'll also find out about, and treat, skin conditions and disorders. Hair removal techniques and learning how to perform facials are also included in training.
- **Business:** Training will teach you how to build a clientele and brand yourself and your business. You'll also find out how to manage business finances and how to become an entrepreneur.

As you can see, you'll likely finish cosmetology school with a broad base of knowledge. Cosmetology school provides a mix of classroom learning and hands-on learning, so you'll get some on-the-job training.

You'll need a certain number of hours of training before you'll be eligible to take your licensing exam. Usually, it's somewhere between 1,400 and 1,600 hours, depending on the state you live in. You can check your state's requirements to find out how many hours you'll need for the area that you live in.

You'll most likely need to be at least 18 years old to enroll in cosmetology school, and have your high school diploma or GED.

COMMUNITY COLLEGE

Community college is another option for aspiring cosmetologists. Many community colleges offer programs in cosmetology so explore the colleges in your area to see whether they do. Such programs generally allow you to earn either an associate's degree in cosmetology or a certificate in cosmetology or in a particular part of the cosmetology field. The difference between the two is often the number of hours required to complete the program. In some cases, the associate's degree includes general education (GE) requirements, whereas the certificate doesn't. The GE requirements can be useful if you think you may want to pursue a four-year degree at some point.

The United States doesn't have any four-year programs specifically in cosmetology, but there are some related degrees you might ultimately be interested in. For example, the Fashion Institute of Design & Merchandising in Los Angeles offers a bachelor's degree in beauty marketing and product development and one in beauty business management. If you think you might someday want to pursue a four-year degree, earning your associate's degree in cosmetology is a good idea.

Community college can be a great place to develop your skills and widen your friendship group.

The associate's degree may also offer courses in business and marketing that aren't offered at the cosmetology school. These can be particularly helpful if you hope to someday have your own business.

WHICH ROUTE SHOULD YOU CHOOSE?

Which route to take is a very personal decision and something only you can decide. However, one thing to keep in mind about cosmetology schools is that they're often branded, such as Paul Mitchell. Because of that, all your experience will be with Paul Mitchell techniques and products. There's nothing wrong with that, and you can certainly adapt when you get out of school and start working. However, it is something to keep in mind.

THE BEAUTY BAG: TOOLS YOU'LL NEED FOR SCHOOL

At many cosmetology schools, you're expected to bring your own training kit. Some schools will provide training kits, but many don't. So expect to need to bring the following tools:

- **Hairstyling tools:** clippers, scissors, hairdryer, curling irons, brushes, and combs, and possibly a mannequin (dummy) head for practicing
- **Manicure tools:** nail clippers, files, and cuticle trimmers
- **Skincare tools:** tweezers, gloves, headbands, and waxing materials
- **Makeup products:** primer, foundation, powder, concealer, bronzer, blush, a contouring palette, eyebrow pencils, mascara, eyeliner, makeup brushes, and false eyelashes

Often, you'll have to provide your own beauty tools. This is not a small expense, but on the upside, you get to choose the tools you like.

Try to talk to people who've gone through cosmetology school and those who've done a community college program. See what they liked and didn't like about the path they chose.

OTHER BENEFITS

Cosmetology school is often shorter in duration than community college, so you'll finish your education more quickly. Also, many cosmetologists say that the real learning happens after you finish cosmetology school or community college. They believe the goal of cosmetology school or community college is to prepare you for your licensing exams, which is indeed important. If you don't pass the exam, you can't work in the field. But a lot of the more practical learning takes place after you are licensed and can start working in a salon with paying customers.

TALK TO PEOPLE

If you can, talk to people who have attended cosmetology school in your area and those who have attended the community college program. Ask whether they're satisfied with the training they received and whether they would

PRO TIP: START WHERE YOU WANT TO BE

Cosmetologists have said that if you can get any job in the salon or spa where you ultimately want to work, do it. Even if the job is sweeping up or just answering the phone. Never underestimate the value of networking. If you work in the salon while you're studying to get your license, for example, you can make connections that could lead to a job as a stylist or makeup artist or aesthetician after you pass your exam. It pays to be connected!

recommend a different path in retrospect. See, too, if you can get information from either school on the rate of students who pass their state licensing exams.

HOW MUCH SCHOOLING?

As mentioned, you need to fulfill a certain number of hours of education before you can take your licensing exam. However, if you only want to become licensed in a specific part of the cosmetology field (rather than having a standard cosmetology license), you can do that, and the number of training hours will be fewer. For example, the state of Arizona requires you to have 1,450 training hours before you can take your exam for your cosmetology license. But if you want a license just to be a nail technician, for example, the required training hours are just 500.

GETTING AN APPRENTICESHIP

In some states, you can do an apprenticeship instead of a formal cosmetology program. You'll still need to make sure you're well-prepared for the state licensing exam, though, so keep that in mind when exploring the possibility of doing an apprenticeship. You'll get lots of hands-on learning, but you might struggle more with preparation for the licensing exam, depending on the state's requirements for classroom education. The requirements for apprenticeships vary based on state, so you'll need to look it up for your location.

Look at the requirements for licensing exams in your state to determine how many hours you'll need to put in before you can become licensed in your chosen part of the field.

GET LICENSED

In all 50 states, you have to be licensed to work in the cosmetology fields. The licensing requirements vary by state, but they usually include factors such as:

- **Minimum age:** The minimum age is usually between 16 and 18.
- **Education:** Most states require a high school diploma or GED, and most have requirements about board-approved training programs beyond high school.
- **Examination:** All states have examinations you must pass. They may be written exams on theory and procedures, practical exams on skills, and/or written exams on state regulations.
- **Infectious disease training:** Some states require specific training on preventing the transmission of infectious diseases such as HIV/AIDS.
- **Continuing education:** Most states require you to do a certain amount of continuing education to satisfy requirements when you renew your license. This isn't a bad thing, as it allows you to keep up on the newest developments and trends in the industry.

It's important to note that licensing is not permanent. That means regardless of where you work or in what part of the field, you'll need to renew your license periodically. Requirements vary by state, so you can look it up for your location.

PRO TIP: START AS AN EMPLOYEE

While many cosmetologists are self-employed, it's recommended by those in the field that you consider starting your career by working at an established business. The learning curve in any profession is steepest at the beginning. For that reason, it's helpful not to have to worry about running a business while you're getting used to the job. Also, if you spend a few years working in a salon or spa owned by someone else, you have time to network and build up a potential client base. If you're a hairdresser, for example, people will get to like the way you cut, color, and style their hair. They are then likely to follow you if you move from where you are to somewhere else in the area. That means when you undertake the somewhat daunting task of starting your own business, you may already have a client base to get you going.

GET EXPERIENCE

"I'm glad I started my career working for a salon. It meant I got the experience I needed in the business to be able to branch out on my own now. It also meant I got to work as part of a great team for a while."

If you are passionate about healthy and beautiful skin, working as an aesthetician could be a good career for you.

Being a barber can be both a well-paid and rewarding job.

Hopefully, everything you've learned so far sounds good. And, as you can see, there are many options for what path to take to make your dream of becoming a cosmetologist come true. In the next chapter, you'll learn more about the work environment you can expect when working in the cosmetology field.

STARTING EARLY

The cosmetology field is somewhat unique in that you may be able to start working toward your career while you're still in high school. Some vocational high schools offer cosmetology programs, and some community colleges will also admit high school students into their cosmetology programs. So if you're eager to get started, there are plenty of available options.

BUSTING MYTHS: NOT JUST FOR WOMEN

Men are becoming increasingly well represented in the cosmetology field—and not just as barbers. Top makeup artists and stylists are sometimes men, too.

Years ago, most career fields were dominated by men. However, women dominated in just a few areas. They were mainly secretaries, nurses, teachers, and cosmetologists. That is no longer the case. While women still make up the majority of professionals in the beauty industry, men represent a significant number. Depending on the source you consult, anywhere from 7 percent to 19 percent of professionals in the beauty industry are male.

WHY AREN'T THERE MORE MEN?

Nineteen percent isn't a terrible representation for a career that used to be even more heavily dominated by females, but it still isn't representative of the population. Recent BLS statistics show that 67.9 percent of men are employed versus 55.4 percent of women. If this high number of men are in work, why are they underrepresented in the cosmetology field?

Stigma is likely part of it. In the past, working on makeup and nails in particular were considered "women's work." Hairstyling was a little less so, since men often visited male barbers for their haircuts. In fact, today, many of the most highly sought-after hairdressers in the business are male. However, for generations, cosmetology has been considered a female industry.

MEN BREAKING DOWN THE BARRIERS

Luckily, there are several boundary-breakers out there who are helping to move the needle in both parts of the industry. Wayne Goss is a good example. Goss suffered from acne as a teen. His attempts to cover his acne with makeup led him to develop a strong interest in it. He learned techniques by reading books when the Internet was still quite new and YouTube and TikTok tutorials didn't exist. He then trained professionally as a makeup artist, and in 2009 launched his YouTube channel, providing user-friendly tutorials on how to do makeup. He has since launched his own line of makeup brushes. His YouTube channels continue to be extremely popular, and his 4 million subscribers find him at @WayneGoss on YouTube or on Instagram at @gossmakeupartist.

WOMEN BREAKING DOWN THE BARRIERS

It is interesting to note that most high-level executives of beauty companies are male. So while men are underrepresented at the lower levels of the industry, women are underrepresented at the top. However, things are changing.

Makeup artist Pat McGrath started her working life as a receptionist while working alongside renowned designers in London, England. All the while, she cultivated her skills as a makeup artist. In 1999, she collaborated with Giorgio Armani on a line of cosmetics, and from there her career exploded. She launched the Pat McGrath Labs beauty products line in 2015, which is now valued at more than $1 billion. McGrath is known for a bold, adventurous style of makeup artistry, and she comments that she loves being a makeup artist because it is always changing and never boring.

MEN TOO

"I was worried about going into cosmetology, but on my program there were a lot of guys as well as women. And I now work in a salon that has several male employees."

CHAPTER 3

Different Jobs and Different Environments

In this chapter, we'll discuss the numerous different work environments you may have as a cosmetologist. The term "work environment" describes the physical space, working conditions, and general approach that is part of a job. Work environment impacts how we feel at work and whether we enjoy our job, so it's an important consideration as you think about your future career. As a cosmetologist, there will be several different options available as work environments, so you're sure to find one that suits you.

MAIN ROLES TO CHOOSE FROM

There are many jobs you can do in the cosmetology industry, but in terms of work environment they can be roughly divided into a few main categories, as follows:

- Hairdresser
- Aesthetician
- Makeup artist
- Nail technician

Let's look more closely at the environments that are associated with each.

WORKING AS A HAIRDRESSER

Hairdressers cut, color, treat, and style hair. They are also sometimes called hairstylists. Some say that hairstylists focus solely on styling, whereas hairdressers also cut, color, and treat hair. So you may hear the terms used interchangeably, but in this book we'll use the more inclusive term "hairdresser."

Hairdressers work in a variety of environments. Some work for a salon or spa where they report to a boss, and others rent a station in a salon but act as their own boss.

All hairdressers can color hair, but some specialize in coloring and, as such, can often charge a higher fee for their services.

As a hairdresser, you could work in salons or spas, or in freelance settings, such as a shop set up in your home. You would cut, color, and style clients' hair based on each client's wishes and your own expertise. Often clients have a general idea of what they're looking for, and you would provide guidance about how that might work on their hair. Someone with thin, limp hair, for example, is going to have a tough time achieving beachy waves. It would be your job to let clients know when their expectations may not be realistic or what it would take to achieve them.

Hairdressers are also colorists, which involves many different types of color services. They include all-over color, highlights, lowlights, and balayage. You could also carry out other types of hair treatments to help improve the appearance and health of your clients' hair. These treatments include scalp massage, keratin treatment, or deep conditioning. Hairdressers provide suggestions, too, for products clients can use at home to maintain their hair's health and appearance. And you would also have the less exciting, but very important, job of regularly cleaning your workstation. You would also need to sanitize your tools and equipment to meet safety and hygiene standards.

If you choose to work in a salon, you will generally have a dedicated workstation that holds all your tools and haircare products. You may be employed by the salon or may simply rent the workstation. If you are employed by the salon, you would typically be paid by the salon. Appointments may be booked by the salon, too. If you simply rent a station at a salon, you would need to handle your own bookings, scheduling, and payments.

QUALIFICATIONS AND TRAINING

You'll need a high school diploma or GED to become a hairdresser. In addition, you'll need to have completed a training program, either through a cosmetology school or through a community college. It may also be through an apprenticeship, though that depends on your state.

You must pass the examination for your state and become licensed. The exact type of license depends on your state, but it's some level of cosmetology license. Some are called hairdressing licenses, and some states require additional licenses for services such as braiding. But a quick Internet search of "cosmetology license" along with your state name should yield the information for your area.

WHAT'S THE PAY?

According to the BLS, the median hourly wage for hairdressers and barbers in the United States is $16.87 an hour. However, that wage varies greatly based on where you work—both the geographical location and the type of business. A hairdresser at a low-priced chain salon likely isn't going to make a lot of money. But if you work at a high-end salon, you are likely to make much more—and even more if that high-end salon is in a high-priced city such as New York City or San Francisco.

Skilled hairdressers are always in demand and often have a loyal base of clients.

Men are now embracing stylish hair more than they once did. And as a result, high-end barbers and stylists for men are in greater demand.

SUCCESS STORIES

Jason Schneidman is a hairdresser to the stars, styling the hair of celebrities such as actor Rob Lowe and musicians Bruno Mars and Mark Ronson. However, Schneidman is also a hairdresser to people experiencing homelessness and addiction. It is his passion project, which he funds by selling his own line of exclusive haircare products and with the money he earns as a hairdresser to the stars.

Schneidman himself struggled with addiction, realizing 20 years ago that his own dependence on crack cocaine was going to cost him his life. So he started going to meetings to support his sobriety, and met a man who had styled actress Jennifer Aniston's hair. Schneidman went to rehab and worked in the man's salon, learning everything he could from him. That launched his career as a celebrity hairdresser. However, he wanted to help others who have struggled with the same path he was going down, so he began offering free haircuts to unhoused people and building relationships with them. He helps those who express a willingness to start down the path to recovery to enrol on a program through a nonprofit foundation he created called California Born. For the ones who aren't yet ready to get into rehabilitation, he simply cuts their hair, listens to them, and builds a relationship. He knows they'll come to him when they're ready—and he'll be waiting. You can learn more about Schneidman's foundation at Californiaborn.com, and he's on Instagram as @themensgroomer.

A BEAUTIFUL JOB: BEING AN AESTHETICIAN

Aestheticians work as skincare professionals. Of course, makeup artists work on skin too, but makeup artists apply makeup, whereas aestheticians focus more on the health of a person's skin.

Aestheticians often work in salons or spas, but they also work in doctor's offices. Certain types of skin damage and skin health issues can be addressed by an aesthetician and don't require a dermatologist. For that reason, many medical practices employ aestheticians.

As an aesthetician you would recommend skincare products to clients based on their skin health and skincare needs. However, you would also perform superficial cosmetic procedures. The word "superficial" is key here: it refers to only the topmost layers of skin. Aestheticians are not allowed to perform so-called "invasive" procedures that go beyond the top layer of skin. So if a skincare problem needs further intervention, such as a small cyst that needs to be removed with a scalpel, the client must be referred to a dermatologist. But for surgical treatments that are noninvasive, such as chemical peels, aestheticians are allowed to perform the treatment.

Aestheticians can also offer treatments such as exfoliations and perform superficial extractions of blemishes like blackheads.

Aestheticians carry out facials and also offer more advanced facial treatments such as laser resurfacing and rejuvenation, light therapy, and microdermabrasion. Waxing is also a regularly performed treatment.

QUALIFICATIONS AND TRAINING

To work as an aesthetician, you'll need a high school diploma or GED. You must also complete an educational program—that can be either at a cosmetology school or at a community college. Typically, aestheticians also do an internship to get hands-on experience.

In every state, aestheticians must also pass a state licensing exam that tests them on aesthetics practices and scientific concepts. The requirements to take the licensing exam vary by state. A few states also offer advanced licenses that allow aestheticians to do more advanced procedures.

There is a key difference between licensing and certification where aestheticians are concerned. Some organizations, including the National Coalition of Estheticians Association (NCEA), provide aestheticians with certifications. This can be beneficial when trying to find work or when establishing your own business, for example. However, this certification is not a license to practice—it is merely a certification showing mastery in various aspects of the field. You still need to get a state license before you can legally practice in the field.

WHAT'S THE PAY?

The average salary for aestheticians varies by location and the setting you work in. However, a ballpark average figure across all states is somewhere in the mid-to-high $30,000 range, depending on which source you consult. It's worth noting that typically aestheticians who work in medical offices make more than aestheticians who work in salons and spas. The treatments offered in medical offices generally cost more and therefore the earning capacity in those environments tends to be greater than elsewhere.

There is a wealth of creativity in being a makeup artist, and it's exciting to see how dramatically you can change a person's look.

LIFE AS A MAKEUP ARTIST

Makeup artists are just that—artists. Their canvas is their client's face. Sometimes, their work involves bringing out the best features in a person's face and minimizing imperfections or flaws. Other times, it involves doing creative makeup for a movie or a fashion show.

As a makeup artist, you could work out of a salon or a spa, and may do makeup for special events such as weddings and proms. Some makeup artists work on movie, television, or theater sets. Others work at fashion shows. If you were to work on movie, television, theater, or fashion sets, your "office" would be mobile. You would frequently move between locations with your tools. If you were to work in a salon or spa, you would have a more stable location.

If you worked out of a salon or spa, you would typically work on your own. Your only work as part of a team would be if your client wanted other salon or spa services that are performed by other professionals. If you worked in film, television, theater, or fashion, on the other hand, you would often work as part of a makeup team. The makeup required for such projects can take a long time, depending on the production—for example, if making up someone for a period drama or a horror movie. Other times, the makeup must be created quickly, such as when models are working the runway at a fashion show and need a quick touchup.

If working in film, television, theater, or fashion, you would generally be a freelance or independent contractor. You'd handle your own pay, taxes, and bookings. If you worked as part of a salon or spa, you might be an independent contractor. However, you might also be an employee of the salon or spa. That means you'd be issued a paycheck that already has taxes subtracted from it, and the employer may offer you other benefits such as health insurance and possibly retirement plans too.

QUALIFICATIONS AND TRAINING

You'll need a high school diploma or GED to be a makeup artist. Beyond that, the requirements vary based on where you work and what you plan to do. Some states require you to have a makeup artistry license, which is a specialized license just for that field. Other states require you to have a full cosmetology license. And some states don't require you to have any license to be a makeup artist. You can look up the licensing requirements for your state to determine what you'll need.

Some makeup artists do makeup for special events, such as weddings, and others work in the entertainment industry.

TRAINING IS IMPORTANT

Even if you plan to work in a state that doesn't require licensing, it's good to get training in the field. You may be quite good at makeup application just from your own experimenting and watching expert tutorials on TikTok, Instagram, or YouTube. However, there's still more to be learned, and knowing as much as you possibly can about the field will only help you when you look for jobs. In addition, if you hope to work in areas such as film or television, you'll likely need advanced training to be considered for hire.

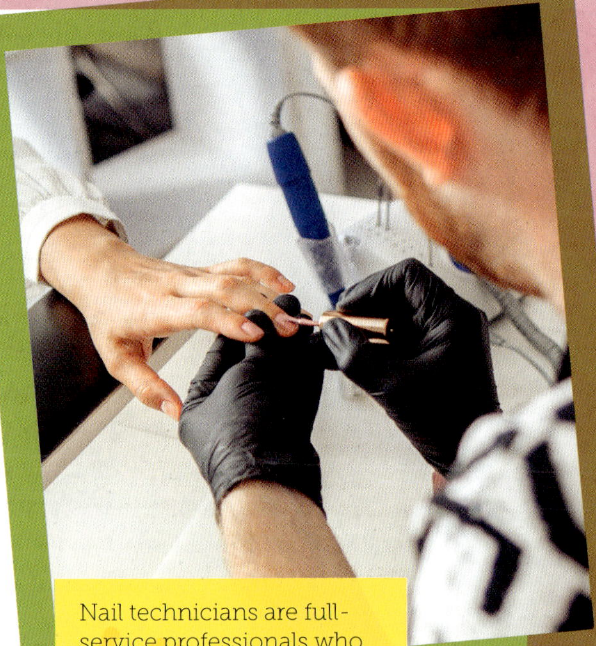

Nail technicians are full-service professionals who not only do manicures and pedicures but also nail art.

WHAT'S THE PAY?

Makeup artistry pays quite well in the field of cosmetology. Pay varies greatly by location, experience, and where you work. The average annual salary across the United States is about $52,605.

WORKING AS A NAIL TECHNICIAN

The term manicurist is often used when talking about nail technicians, but nail technician is a more inclusive term. That is because nail technicians perform manicures and pedicures, but they also do nail artistry. A manicure or pedicure includes shaping the nails, trimming cuticles, softening callouses, and removing rough skin. It includes moisturizing the hands and feet, as well as applying polish to fingernails and toenails. As a nail technician you would carry out this work, but you would also be a nail artist. You might apply gel or acrylic finish to nails, but you could also create fancy patterns and custom designs on a client's nails.

Nail technicians are also trained to understand nail anatomy and health, and you could advise clients on issues such as treating nail fungus or brittle nails. In this job, you would need to thoroughly sanitize all tools and your work area to ensure that you preserve the health of your clients' nails.

QUALIFICATIONS AND TRAINING

You need a high school diploma or GED to be a nail technician. In addition, you need training in a cosmetology program or a specific nail technician program. This will help you pass the exam to be licensed as a nail technician, which is required in every state. Each state's requirements for the nail technician license vary, so check your state to see what is involved. But you'll need to find some type of training program, usually through a cosmetology school or community college, and pass the licensing exam.

WHAT'S THE PAY?

According to the BLS, the median hourly wage for nail technicians is $16.47 per hour. However, nail salon owners make more money, so there is the possibility to earn a much higher salary, depending on your ultimate career goals.

IT HELPS TO BE A PEOPLE PERSON

"It helps if you like talking to people—and, luckily, I do! Clients say they come to me for my nail work, but also for my company."

Nail technicians might do simple acrylic or gel nails, but some also do really elaborate nail artistry.

CHAPTER 4

Specialized Jobs in Cosmetology

In the previous chapter, we discussed the major types of work environments for the four main categories of cosmetologists: hairdressers, makeup artists, aestheticians, and nail technicians. However, within all those work environments you can also explore more specialized areas of the industry. In this chapter, we'll do just that and take a look at some specialized jobs within the cosmetology field.

WORKING AS A BARBER

Barbers are hair professionals who specialize in men's hair. They wash, cut, and style hair. They may also trim beards and mustaches, fit hairpieces, and shave a person's head or facial hair. Barbers can also carry out perm and coloring services, as well as wax treatments.

If you worked as a barber, it would most likely be in a barbershop. There, you might be employed by the shop owner, or you could be self-employed and just rent a station in the shop. However, some barbers also work freelance, styling celebrities. Some work in the military, where they cut hair for members of the forces.

Barber shops used to be made up entirely of male barbers, but today, female barbers are becoming far more common.

Interestingly, in most states only barbers (and not hairdressers) are licensed to use a razor to cut hair.

Some barbers work in places such as nursing homes, providing haircuts for elderly or sick patients who are unable to travel to salons.

QUALIFICATIONS AND TRAINING

Becoming a barber requires the same training as becoming a hairdresser. You must have a high school diploma or GED. You'll also need training in a cosmetology school or community college to prepare you for state licensing exams. The requirements for licensing vary by state, but all states require you have a license to operate as a barber.

WHAT'S THE PAY?

According to the BLS, the median average salary in the United States for barbers is around $36,100. However, the pay varies by state and by what sector of the industry you work in. Celebrity barbers obviously make a lot more than barbers who work in standard salons—and some famous barbers command high fees for their work. In general, the highest wages for barbers are found in Washington, Texas, New York, Virginia, and a handful of other states scattered around the country.

HAIR COLOR SPECIALIST

Hair color specialists, or colorists as they're often called, specialize in coloring hair. In this role you would cut and style hair as well, but to do so you will have spent years learning about permanent and semipermanent hair color. You'd learn what color will look good with a client's skin tone and how to get the shade the client wants. Storebought DIY color kits can result in dreadful color—reds can turn out brassy and too orange, and blondes don't always yield the desired results when being put on darker base hair colors. Colorists know how to make the color work for each client—and what will be most flattering for them.

Hair color can be all-over, highlights, lowlights, a combination of high- and lowlights, or balayage. Colorists can create all these different looks.

CHEMISTRY AND COLOR

As a colorist, you'd also know how to achieve extreme hair color changes, for example, going from dark brown to platinum blonde. Such a dramatic change usually takes multiple treatments, but hair color specialists know how to make it happen. How? They know a lot about hair chemistry and what it will take to change hair from one color to another.

QUALIFICATIONS AND TRAINING

You'll need a high school diploma or GED to be a hair color specialist. You'll also need training at a cosmetology school or community college program (or possibly an apprenticeship, depending on the requirements of your state). You will need to pass the state licensing exam, too. The requirements for the exam vary depending on your state.

WHAT'S THE PAY?

The pay as a hired color specialist can be good. Estimated average salaries vary widely depending on where you live, but Glassdoor reports the average annual salary for hair colorists at around $69,274. In cities where appearance is heavily valued, such as around the area of Los Angeles where celebrities live and work, the pay can be significantly higher.

WORKING IN TELEVISION AND THE MOVIES

On a movie or television set, your work as a makeup artist might simply be maximizing the actors' best features and minimizing flaws. However, even those changes require an approach different from other types of makeup. Cameras and lighting can alter a person's appearance subtly, and you'd need to take that into account when making your client look their best. Makeup artists on television or movie sets may also have to alter an actor's appearance significantly. Sometimes, you'd need to age them for a role. That involves creating wrinkles and possibly using prosthetics to mimic the look of an older individual. And sometimes, you would need to completely transform the person's appearance, such as in movies like *Avatar* and other science-fiction or fantasy worlds.

Movie or television makeup artists need to be able to create unusual looks for science-fiction movies.

WORKING AS A TEAM

A makeup artist might have to fulfill all roles on a smaller, lower-budget production. However, on bigger movie or television sets, you'd often work as part of a team. This team is generally led by the key makeup artist. They create the makeup for the lead actors and delegate other tasks to the rest of the crew. The key makeup artist usually develops the overall look of makeup for the production, too, which helps to ensure consistency between actors.

Makeup artists work under the key makeup artist and often do the makeup for the non-lead actors and supporting actors. Makeup assistants help the makeup artists and key makeup artists with whatever they need. And special effects makeup artists create the unusual looks that some characters require. That could be makeup for zombie characters or aliens. They create beaten or bloodied characters, and characters who are different ages from the actors portraying them.

QUALIFICATIONS AND TRAINING

You need a high school diploma or GED to be a movie makeup artist. You also will likely want to attend a cosmetology school or community college program that has a specialization in movie makeup. You can also earn a bachelor's degree in theater or a related field as your entry into this line of work.

Makeup assistants may help with applying makeup to both actors' faces and bodies.

In the movie and television industry, makeup artistry sometimes means making up a person with wounds or unattractive features.

Whether you need to be licensed depends on the state you work in. Some states require you to have a cosmetologist license. Some require only a makeup artist-specific license, and some require none. You can look up the requirements for your state.

There are also some certifications for makeup artists that you might choose to take to expand your knowledge and improve your job prospects. Certifications and licenses can only help you as you look for jobs, and you'll want to be sure to have a good portfolio of your work. Many makeup artists use Instagram or a personal website to showcase their work.

WHAT'S THE PAY?

It's difficult to determine the exact average pay for movie or television makeup artists. That is because many sources put them into the same category as theatrical makeup artists, who typically make less. But in general, makeup artists in the movie and television industry appear to make around $75,000 per year. That is a very good salary in the cosmetology field. However, keep in mind that this is a competitive area of the industry, and you'll need to be able to work in an area of the country where movies and television shows are regularly produced.

EYELASH AND BROW SPECIALIST

This job goes by several different titles: eyelash specialist, eyebrow technician, lash and brow specialist, lash stylist, and so on. There are many names, but in this book, we're going to talk about a professional who works on both lashes and brows. You can always investigate further if you're interested in specializing in one or the other, or in a specific treatment type.

Eyelash and brow specialists carry out treatments that shape and maintain eyelashes and eyebrows. There are many treatments that people have for their lashes and brows. They include tweezing, eyebrow threading, and microblading. Brow tints, waxing, and lash perming are also part of the range. So too are lash extensions, lash lifts, and lash tints.

QUALIFICATIONS AND TRAINING

You'll need a high school diploma or GED to become an eyelash and brow specialist. You'll need to have an aesthetician license or a cosmetology license in most states, so will need to have completed an educational program either at a cosmetology school or at a community college.

A good lash and brow specialist can transform a person's appearance.

You'll have to pass the state licensing exam for aestheticians or cosmetologists, depending on your state. The requirements to take the licensing exam vary by state, so you will need to check what is applicable for your area.

Each state has its own rules about what procedures you can do, too. Certain states don't allow certain procedures. For example, eyelash and eyebrow tinting wasn't always allowed in California because the US Food and Drug Administration (FDA) hadn't approved the dyes for use around the eyes. It was recently approved, but you do have to be aware of what procedures are and are not allowed in your state.

Microblading is the exception to the general aesthetician or cosmetologist license rule. Microblading is technically tattooing, so many states require you to have an applicable tattoo license and/or certification. If you are interested in microblading, you can look up the particular licensing requirements for your state.

WHAT'S THE PAY?

The average pay for this career is difficult to establish because it's often split into multiple different jobs. It also varies by location and by the type of salon, spa, or office you work in. But in general, eyelash and brow technicians typically make an average annual salary in the region of $50,000.

LET'S TALK ABOUT TAXES

If you're hired as a regular employee for a company, they'll take taxes out of your paycheck. But as a cosmetologist, you may be self-employed or employed as a contractor. On the surface, it looks like you get a higher paycheck if you're self-employed or employed as a contractor—and you often do. However, that's because your employer doesn't have to pay for insurance or taxes for you, so you must pay for those yourself. In addition to paying the state and federal taxes that an employer typically takes out, you also must pay a 15.3 percent self-employment tax. That goes toward covering what an employer would have paid into Medicare and Social Security for you. That 15.3 percent isn't insignificant, so you'll want to think about that when you consider which part of the cosmetology field you ultimately want to pursue.

CHANGING LOOKS

"I like working on brows and lashes. It's really precise work and it's amazing to see how dramatically you can change someone's look by altering just these two areas."

CHAPTER 5

Other Routes into the Industry

We've talked about the different work environments in the cosmetology field as well as some common and more specialized jobs in the industry. But there are many other jobs available for people interested in working in the cosmetology field. This chapter will highlight a few more you might not have thought of.

WORKING AS A CURL SPECIALIST

Also called a curly hair specialist, curl specialists are hairdressers who specialize in curly hair. This type of hair is notoriously difficult to cut and style if you're not used to it. For that reason, some hairdressers have created a niche part of the field that handles only curly hair. Some curly hair specialists follow specialized training protocols, such as the Curly Girl Method or those created by Curly Hair Artistry. Others don't necessarily follow one special method, but they have extensive experience in dealing with curly hair. They know the best products to use for different types of curls. (If you don't have curls, you might not know that there are specific numbers assigned for curl

For people with curly hair, the services of a curl specialist are invaluable.

types and textures. Different numbers require different treatments and methods.) Specialists know, for example, that you never use a brush on curly hair. Instead, you detangle with fingers when hair is wet and conditioned.

Some curly hair specialists also work specifically on ethnic hair. Black or biracial people have a very specific type of hair and curls that require someone very knowledgeable about the hair type. Black or ethnic salons are therefore popular with people who have these types of hair and want to go to a specialist who knows how to work with the hair.

The structure of ethnic hair is different from that of nonethnic hair. As a curl specialist, knowing how to properly care for and cut ethnic hair is very important.

QUALIFICATIONS AND TRAINING

You'll need a high school diploma or GED to become a curl specialist. In addition, you'll need to have completed a training program, either through a cosmetology school or through a community college. You may also be able to train through an apprenticeship, though that depends on your state. You must pass the examination for your state and become licensed. The exact type of license depends on your state, but it's some level of cosmetology license. (Some are called hairdressing licenses, and some states require additional licenses for services like braiding.)

There are specific certification programs for working with curly hair that aren't required but that will help you with your knowledge. They will also boost your credibility as a curl specialist. Some of these certification programs include Rëzo, Sisterlocks, and Cut It Kinky.

WHAT'S THE PAY?

Not surprisingly, higher-end salons yield higher salaries. However, in general, curl specialists make more than other hairdressers because the market supports it. People with curly hair are typically willing to pay more for a good haircut by someone who really knows how to work with their hair. So if curls are your thing, this is a lucrative part of the field to get into.

WORKING AS A CONTENT CREATOR

A book about cosmetology wouldn't be complete without discussing a recent, but viable, career choice: content creator. A lot of people interested in hair, makeup, and skincare turn to social media for how-to tutorials and reviews of beauty products. As such, many cosmetologists have found fame and careers as content creators.

Content creators are people who consistently create content about a specific topic for a particular audience. For example, someone who is exceptionally skilled at makeup artistry might create how-to videos for YouTube, Instagram, TikTok, or other platforms. They are skilled in whatever type of content they create, but they are also skilled marketers. They know how to brand and promote themselves.

If you worked as a content creator you could earn money in several ways. Advertising revenue is one. If you're popular enough on a particular platform, businesses will want to advertise on your channel. Sponsorships and brand partnerships are another way content creators can earn money. Some also sell merchandise if they've created a product line. And some offer paid subscriptions to their content channel or raise money through fan funding.

Many content creators have made a living for themselves posting beauty tutorials on social media.

Content creation can be lucrative—if you can do it well, there is a lot of money to be made in this area.

QUALIFICATIONS AND TRAINING

There aren't necessarily specific requirements for becoming a content creator. You don't need any type of license to have a YouTube channel or an Instagram account, for example. However, you do need to be good at what you do and have a personality that draws in viewers.

WHAT'S THE PAY?

The pay of a content creator is difficult to gauge because it is so variable. It depends on the type of content created, the platforms used, the number of followers, and more. For example, part of the pay structure on Instagram takes into account how much your followers interact with your posts. You might have a lot of followers, but if they just scroll on by without liking or commenting on your posts, you'll make less money than if you have followers who actively interact on your posts. Engagement is key!

There is, however, huge potential in this area. The top five beauty influencers creating content on Instagram, YouTube, and TikTok make combined earnings per post of anywhere from $99,500 to $196,000 in a year. Did you catch the *per post* part of that? So yes, there's money to be made in content creation if you create good content and you know how to market it with maximum effect.

One factor to bear in mind is that the field of content creation is very new. For that reason it's hard to say what the staying power will be. Ten years ago, blogging was big; now blogs are largely a thing of the past, and content creation is mostly on social media platforms. So the landscape in this fast-moving industry can change quickly. It pays to keep that in mind if you intend to follow this route as a career.

CHAPTER 6

Your Career Future

When you're thinking about your career, you need to consider what that career might look like in the future. There's no way to know for sure what the future holds. However, you can take the information available today and draw some conclusions. According to the BLS, job growth for cosmetologists is expected to be significant in the coming decade. That means if you are interested in cosmetology, the future looks bright.

UPCOMING NEW TECHNOLOGIES

Those who are best poised to build a strong career in cosmetology in the future are those who keep up on the latest developments in the field. You might not immediately think of technology when you think of the future of cosmetology (more beauty trends, perhaps), but indeed technology does play a role in the future of the cosmetology field.

SKINCARE AND HAIRCARE ANALYSIS

One advancement in the field of aesthetics is skincare analysis. Facial recognition software and other specialized technologies can perform skin assessments and give personalized feedback for recommendations on skincare. This can be helpful for people with issues such as acne, wrinkles, or dark spots. Moles are a separate issue. Concerning moles always need to be looked at by a doctor to screen for skin cancers.

Similarly, there are smart haircare devices that analyze the condition of a person's scalp and hair. They then recommend products that will work best based on that person's individual scalp and hair health.

A NEW REALITY

When you look in the mirror, you're looking at the real world —a reflection of yourself, just as you are. But augmented reality (AR) tools can superimpose an image on top of your reflection.

Skincare and haircare analysis is a relatively new and growing part of the cosmetology field.

Artificial intelligence (AI) is providing tools to help make cosmetologists even more effective at their jobs.

AR superimposes a computer-generated image on a user's view of the real world. So if you would like to see how a particular hairstyle or shade of lipstick might look on you, an AR tool could help you do that.

A NEW TYPE OF INTELLIGENCE

AI is affecting nearly every industry, and that includes the beauty industry. AI analyzes huge amounts of data to identify trends and return conclusions. For example, if you asked AI what the best shampoo for 2A curly hair is, it would search the Internet for every shampoo recommendation for 2A curly hair and return a list of the best results. It's like doing a Google search, only greatly amplified and far more efficient. When you get a list of Google results, you must wade through them. But AI does this work for you and gives you an answer in moments. AI is also being used alongside biotechnology advancements to create "clean," sustainable products for consumers who want to make earth-friendly purchases while looking good.

HOW DOES TECHNOLOGY HELP ME?

You might wonder how all the innovation we've just discussed can help you as a cosmetologist. After all, if customers can ask AI bots for beauty recommendations, what need is there for them to talk with stylists? If they can 3-D-print personalized foundation, why do they need to watch tutorials about how to match the right foundation and powder to your skin tone?

First, the average client isn't going to have a 3-D printer readily available that can create their perfect personalized foundation. But second, technology is not likely to ever replace human knowledge, creativity, and expertise. Sure, AI can scour the Internet in seconds to get answers to questions, but it cannot evaluate those answers. It can tell us five different great shampoos for 2A curly hair, but its responses are only as good as the information available on the Internet—and a lot of that information may not be great.

ALWAYS LEARNING

"It helps to keep up with changes in the industry, like new tech. It keeps you on top of your game, and it's really interesting, too."

Believe it or not, you can now print beauty products, such as personalized shades of foundation, using a 3-D printer.

Good aestheticians are able to listen to the concerns of their clients and provide solutions.

In addition, AI can't touch your 2A curly hair and say, "Yes, you do have 2A hair, but it's a little more coarse than usual 2A hair. So I don't think a typical shampoo for 2A curly hair would be best. I think this other product might work better, and here's why."

Skincare analysis tools and 3-D printing might have created the perfect personalized foundation for a client, but what happens when that client spends their summer working outside, and their skin tone is altered from the constant sun exposure (even with sunscreen)? A good aesthetician can let the client know what to do to adjust for the changes in skin tone.

So a smart cosmetologist will know about all these tools and know how to use them to work in a smarter way. And they'll also recognize that their own expertise in the field can never be matched by technology.

MOVING AHEAD

There is a truly glowing future in cosmetology, so if you want to carve out a career in this field, you are on to a good thing. To get your career off to a great start, look at all the training options available to you, considering what you have learned in this book. Also consider all the many different roles you could pursue. There are so many options to choose from that you'll never be bored in the field, so make the most of this vibrant practical career.

MORE PRACTICAL CAREERS

You can enjoy many different jobs in the cosmetology industry. We've picked out some of them but there are a lot more to choose from too. If none of the jobs on the following pages fit your dream career, turn to pages 62–63. There you'll find links to sites on which you can research even more jobs in the industry.

THEATRICAL MAKEUP ARTIST

Theatrical makeup artists design the makeup to fit a production and apply it to the performers. Theatrical makeup presents a unique challenge because the audience is far from the performers. Makeup needs to be bold enough for the audience to be able to see it, but it shouldn't look clownish and over the top.

Stage lighting plays a big role in how makeup needs to be applied, too. And so too does the character's personality—makeup in a stage production really helps to develop the character. This is especially true in performance art productions, such as mime. But, it's also true in more common types of theater productions, such as musicals and stage shows.

If you love theater and makeup, being a theatrical makeup artist might be a field of interest for you.

Theatrical makeup artists work in theaters, but also in other environments. They include theme parks, cruise ships, and touring dance companies.

Another factor that makes theatrical makeup artistry more challenging is the need for quick touchups and changes to a look. Artists must often make changes very quickly to a character's makeup between scenes. Theatrical makeup artists must be both good at their job—and quick.

QUALIFICATIONS AND TRAINING

You need a high school diploma or GED to be a theatrical makeup artist. You also will likely want to attend a cosmetology school or community college program that has a specialization in theatrical makeup. You can also earn a bachelor's degree in theater or a related field to get into the area.

Whether you need to be licensed depends on the state you'll be working in. Some states require you to have a cosmetologist license. Some require only a makeup artist-specific license, and some require none. You'll have to look up the requirements for your state.

You'll also want to be sure to have a good portfolio of your work. Your portfolio helps show off how great you are at your job and can make all the difference in persuading someone to hire you for a position.

WHAT'S THE PAY?

The pay for theatrical makeup artists varies widely based on where you're working and what type of theatrical makeup work you do. For example, working as a makeup artist for a big show on Broadway pays more than doing makeup for a small-town local theater. But in general, the average annual salary for theatrical makeup artists is about $50,000.

HAIRDRESSING EDUCATOR

If you've worked as a hairdresser and gained a lot of experience, you may eventually want to give back and teach others the career of hairdressing. There are a couple of rewarding ways to achieve this.

First, if there is a particular brand of products you like, you can become affiliated with that brand. So, for example, if you like Aveda products, you could become a hairdressing educator for Aveda. Many of the major beauty brands hire educators, and you can explore whether the ones you like do so. This can be a great way to make connections in the industry, too.

The other option is to teach without having a brand affiliation, or an association with a brand. You can teach at a cosmetology school or a community college, for example, or you can offer classes on your own. The advantage of this is that you're not beholden to using a certain brand or their methods. The disadvantage is that you don't necessarily get the chance to make as many industry connections.

QUALIFICATIONS AND TRAINING

To become a hairdressing educator at a salon or for a brand, you need to be experienced and licensed.

If you want to work as an educator at either a community college or cosmetology school, there may be additional requirements, depending on the school. You can look for job openings at these types of schools in your area to get a picture of what the organizations are looking for.

WHAT'S THE PAY?

Hairdressing educator salaries vary widely based on where you teach and whether it's for a school or with a brand affiliation. However, in general, hairdressing educators make an average of $50,000 per year across the United States.

If you're an experienced hairdresser, you might want to give back to the community by teaching the next generation of hairstylists—and earn a living from doing so.

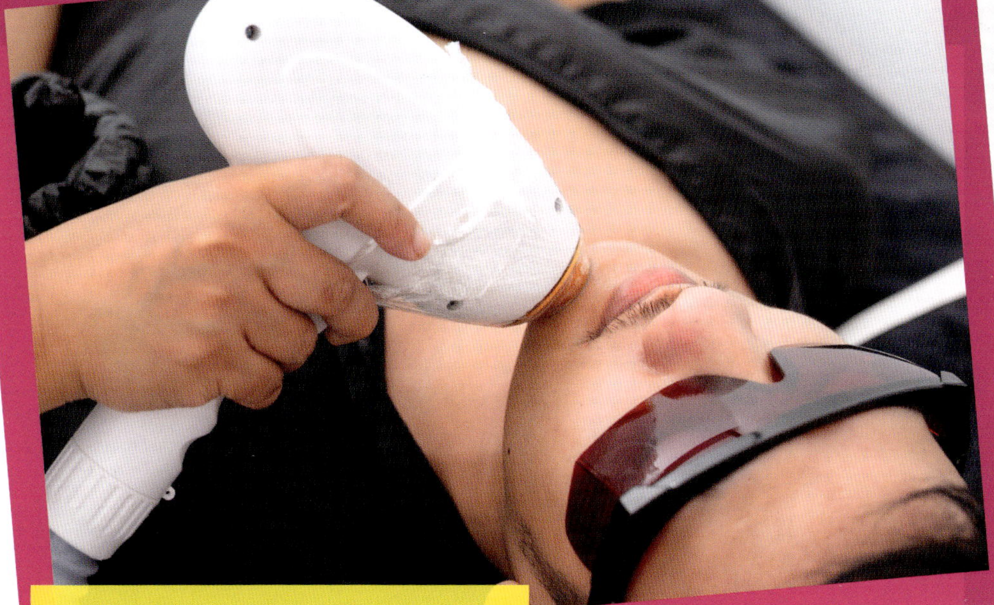

Laser hair removal technicians use lasers to damage hair follicles so the hair does not grow back after it has been removed.

LASER HAIR REMOVAL TECHNICIAN

Working as a laser hair removal technician is a skilled job. Lasers can be harmful if not used correctly. For that reason, laser hair removal technicians need to be properly trained in safety procedures.

QUALIFICATIONS AND TRAINING

Cosmetology programs typically include instruction on laser hair removal, so if you go to a cosmetology school or go through a cosmetology program at a community college, you will likely get the basic training needed to be a laser hair removal technician. There are also some laser hair removal certification programs through which you can earn a certificate in this area without having to complete the full cosmetology program.

Depending on your state, you may be required to get a license to perform laser hair removal. You can research your specific state's requirements. There are also some national certifications you can get if you want to be more competitive in the job market.

WHAT'S THE PAY?

The pay for laser hair removal technicians varies based on where you are located and the type of facility you work in. However, in general, laser hair removal technicians make around $50,000 per year.

WHAT'S NEXT? YOUR CAREER CHECKLIST

We've covered a lot in this book, and you've discovered much about the world of cosmetology. Now let's get to grips with some questions you need to ask and steps you need to take for a career as a cosmetologist.

QUESTIONS TO ASK ABOUT SCHOOLS AND COURSES

- Is the program accredited? (Whether you choose cosmetology school or community college, this is an important question. Accredited programs guarantee that you'll get a quality education. They also look far better to potential employers when applying for jobs than unaccredited programs.)
- What types of training and classes are offered in your program?
- Do you offer specialty certifications in different areas of the field?
- How rigorous is the program? (You need to know how much time to devote to your studies daily. Some people attend community college part time while they work, but some programs may require that you devote yourself to them full time.)
- How much hands-on training does your program allow, compared to classroom learning?
- How much does your program cost, and is financial aid available?

QUESTIONS TO ASK ABOUT APPRENTICESHIPS

- How many hours a week can I expect to work? (You need a certain number of hours to finish an apprenticeship, so this is an important question.)
- What parts of the trade can I expect to learn in an apprenticeship with you?
- Will your program help prepare me for licensing exams?
- What is the pay?

QUESTIONS TO ASK WHEN INTERVIEWING FOR A JOB

- Do you provide opportunities for continued learning?
- Do you require the use of any particular brands of products?

- What is your benefits package? (This typically covers medical insurance, life insurance, vacation time or paid time off, and retirement benefits. By asking this one question about benefits, you'll get the answer to several more questions.)
- What is the salary? (Don't forget this all-important question!)

NAIL THAT INTERVIEW!

Being interviewed can feel stressful. But here are some great steps you can take to ensure your interview goes as well as possible.

- Dress for success! You're going to be working in the beauty industry, so you want to look the part.
- Be clean and well-groomed. Appearances matter in this industry.
- Research the position and company. It's best to go to an interview appearing knowledgeable about your interviewer and what they do.
- Be ready to share your portfolio. Many people have online portfolios, either on Instagram or through a website. Ask the interviewer(s) if you can share your work with them via Instagram, your website, or whatever platform you use for your portfolio.
- Prepare some questions ahead of time. Virtually every interview ends with the employer asking you whether you have any questions for them. Have a question or two prepared.
- Thank the interviewer for their time.
- Follow up with a thank-you note by email or even text afterward.

GLOSSARY

accreditation a certification that a school has met a specific set of standards set by an external group that regulates such schools

apprenticeship a position in which a person works for lower wages while learning a trade from a skilled professional

artificial intelligence (AI) technology designed to imitate human thought

associate's degree a two-year degree awarded to students who have completed a particular course of study at a community college

augmented reality (AR) a technology that creates a composite view by superimposing a computer-generated image on a user's view of the real world

bachelor's degree a degree awarded to students who have completed a particular four-year course of study at a college or university

balayage the freehand painting of highlights on hair, with the goal of achieving a natural gradation toward lightness at the ends of the hair

benefits services provided by employers in addition to wages. May include benefits such as health insurance, life insurance, retirement packages, stock options, and paid time off work

biracial describes a person whose mother and father were of two different ethnic origins

certification a designation that one has completed a course of study (and usually passed a test), and has acquired a certain body of knowledge required in a field

chemical peels the use of chemical solutions on the skin to remove the top layers of the skin

clientele a group of clients

clients people you are completing work for

community college a college that offers various associate's degrees as well as courses that can transfer to a university if a student wishes to pursue a bachelor's degree

custom designs designs that are created for a person according to their preferences

cuticles layers of skin at the base of the fingertips

dermatologist a medical practitioner who specializes in skin and disorders related to it

eco-friendly friendly to the environment

entrepreneur a person who has set up their own business or has plans to do so

freelance working for different companies rather than being permanently employed by a single company

health insurance medical coverage to help a person pay medical bills

interacting engaging with other people

laser resurfacing a technique in which a laser is used to tighten skin, remove lesions, and reduce wrinkles and scars

license a certificate that shows you are legally allowed to do a job

lucrative capable of producing profit

manicure a treatment that involves filing, shaping, and often applying polish to the fingernails

Medicare a federal health insurance system for people over age 65 and some people with disabilities. Everyone must pay into Medicare through their employer taxes or through self-employment tax

microblading a semipermanent makeup technique used to define a person's eyebrows.

microdermabrasion a minimally invasive procedure that resurfaces the skin to treat uneven texture, scars, and signs of age or sun damage

pedicure a treatment that involves filing, shaping, and often applying polish to the toenails

promote to draw attention to something, such as a product or treatment, with the aim of making people aware of it and buy it

prospects the likely future achievements of a person

robot a machine that can replicate human movements

sanitization a process to keep something clean

self-employed working for oneself, not employed by another person or organization

self-employment tax a required tax for contractors or others who are self-employed. It covers Medicare and Social Security taxes that normally are taken out of one's paycheck by an employer

Social Security a government program that provides money to people who are retired or disabled

sponsorships support, sometimes as financial payments, made to support people in their work

student loan a specific type of loan taken out by a person to attend college, university, or trade school

sustainable able to be maintained at a certain rate to avoid depleting natural resources, thereby conserving ecological balance

total compensation package the salary and benefits offered by an employer to an employee. It may include wages, insurance, stock options, bonuses, and more

trade school a school that offers training for a particular career

university an institute of higher learning where students can earn a bachelor's degree and often a master's degree or doctorate degree

vocational related to work, for example, a school offers classes to students to train them for a skilled job or a trade

workers' compensation a type of insurance that covers lost wages and medical costs for employees injured on a job

FIND OUT MORE

BOOKS

Given-Wilson, Rachel and Sally Ganchy. *Your Future as a Cosmetologist* (High-Demand Careers). Rosen Publishing, 2019.

Middleton, Katie. *Color Theory for the Make-Up Artist: Understanding Color and Light for Beauty and Special Effects.* Routledge, 2022.

Potter-Dixon, Lisa. *The Make-Up Manual: Your Beauty Guide for Brows, Eyes, Skin, Lips, and More.* Ryland Peters & Small, 2019.

WEBSITES

Bureau of Labor Statistics (BLS)
Take a look at the BLS website to find out more about the role and outlook for barbers, hairstylists, and cosmetologists:
www.bls.gov/ooh/personal-care-and-service/barbers-hairstylists-and-cosmetologists.htm

Cosmetology-License.com
This site is full of resources about cosmetology services, licensing, schools, careers, and other great information about cosmetology:
www.cosmetology-license.com

Instagram
Many up-and-coming professionals in the cosmetology world are on Instagram. It's a great place to find professionals whose interests match your own and get inspiration from their pages:
www.instagram.com

YouTube

Like Instagram, YouTube has many channels created by people in the cosmetology industry. You can find tutorials and product reviews from your favorite hairstylists, makeup artists, aestheticians, and more: **www.youtube.com**

Publisher's note to educators and parents:
All the websites featured above have been carefully reviewed to ensure that they are suitable for students. However, many websites change often, and we cannot guarantee that a site's future contents will continue to meet our high standards of educational value. Please be advised that students should be closely monitored whenever they access the Internet.

INDEX

ABOUT THE AUTHOR

Cathleen Small has written many books for young people on a wide variety of topics. She hopes this book will show readers that there are many exciting job opportunities for people who are interested in working as a cosmetologist, and that the information provided will help set them on their path toward a perfect practical career.